AI-Powered Productivity:

Maximizing Efficiency and Success in the Modern Workplace

Nena Buenaventura

Disclaimer

This article, *AI-Powered Productivity: Maximizing Efficiency and Success in the Modern Workplace,* provides general information on artificial intelligence tools and practices intended to support productivity and professional growth. It is not a substitute for professional advice or guidance in specific technical, legal, or ethical matters related to AI usage. While we have aimed to present accurate and current information, the landscape of AI technology evolves rapidly, and the effectiveness or availability of specific tools may change over time.

Readers are encouraged to independently verify and evaluate the suitability of any AI tool or technique mentioned, based on their personal or organizational requirements. Additionally, while this article discusses ethical and privacy considerations, users are responsible for ensuring their AI practices comply with applicable laws, policies, and standards. This guide should be used as an introductory resource to inspire further learning, not as an authoritative reference.

Furthermore, this article does not provide legal or financial advice. Readers should consult with qualified professionals for any such advice.

The authors and publishers are not responsible for any consequences arising from the use or misuse of the information presented in this article.

Table of Contents

Preface

In today's rapidly changing world, productivity is no longer just about working harder; it's about working smarter, and artificial intelligence (AI) is one of the most powerful tools that can help us achieve just that. However, for many of us, AI might seem like an intimidating, complex field—something reserved for tech experts and data scientists. Yet, the truth is, AI is for everyone. Whether you're a writer, an artist, a professional managing a busy schedule, or a student eager to learn more effectively, AI has something valuable to offer.

This guide, *AI-Powered Productivity: Maximizing Efficiency and Success in the Modern Workplace,* is here to break down those barriers. It's designed to empower you with practical, accessible ways to make AI an ally in your daily life, no matter your background or level of technical expertise. Imagine a world where repetitive tasks are automated, freeing you to focus on the work that truly matters. Visualize the creativity boost from AI tools that can generate content, design captivating images, and even refine and polish your writing with ease. This book aims to bring that world closer to you, revealing the incredible potential that AI has to streamline your workflow, spark creativity, and help you achieve your goals.

In each chapter, we'll dive into various facets of AI, from understanding how AI enhances productivity to exploring specific tools that can elevate your writing, design work, and project management. You'll learn how to make the most of platforms like ChatGPT and

Grammarly for content creation, Canva for stunning visuals, and Zapier for task automation. We'll also look at the growing field of AI-powered learning tools to help you keep your skills sharp, and we'll address the ethical considerations of using AI so that you can approach this technology with both confidence and integrity.

We understand that adopting new technologies can sometimes feel overwhelming, and that's why this guide is structured to provide you with a clear roadmap, practical tips, and even a glimpse into the future of AI. Each chapter is crafted to encourage you to try new tools, adapt them to your unique needs, and, ultimately, to help you integrate AI in ways that enhance—not complicate—your life.

By the end of this book, you'll feel not only well-informed about the possibilities of AI but also inspired to integrate this powerful technology seamlessly into your work, your learning, and your creative pursuits. *AI-Powered Productivity* is more than just a guide; it's an invitation to step into the future of work with curiosity, enthusiasm, and an empowered mindset.

Introduction

In today's rapidly evolving digital landscape, artificial intelligence (AI) has emerged as a game-changing force, reshaping how individuals and organizations approach productivity and efficiency. AI's transformative power lies in its ability to streamline complex tasks, analyze massive datasets, and even automate creative processes—all of which are revolutionizing industries ranging from finance and healthcare to education and entertainment. As businesses face mounting pressures to adapt quickly, integrate new technologies, and maintain a competitive edge, the use of AI has become essential. Those who harness the potential of AI effectively can amplify their productivity, foster innovation, and ultimately stay ahead in a crowded, fast-paced marketplace.

This guide offers a comprehensive roadmap for those looking to navigate the AI-powered tools and technologies that can enhance daily tasks and contribute to long-term success. By diving into practical applications, readers will learn how to use AI tools to streamline workflow, fuel creativity, and maximize efficiency across various fields. Each chapter delves into different aspects of AI, including tools for writing, content creation, visual design, task management, and skill development, offering actionable strategies to help users make the most of what AI has to offer. Whether you are a beginner exploring AI for the first time or an experienced user seeking new insights, this guide aims to empower you with the knowledge and confidence to incorporate AI seamlessly into your personal and professional life.

This guide is crafted for a wide audience. Students can use AI tools to enhance their research and study processes, enabling them to work smarter, not harder. Writers, both aspiring and seasoned, can unlock new realms of creativity with AI-powered writing aids, which help brainstorm ideas, structure content, and refine prose. Professionals in corporate settings can leverage AI to manage data, optimize workflows, and improve decision-making. Finally, entrepreneurs, faced with the demands of a fast-moving business landscape, can use AI to streamline operations, refine marketing efforts, and gain insights into customer behavior—all essential components of a successful modern business strategy.

In essence, *AI-Powered Productivity: Maximizing Efficiency and Success in the Modern Workplace* is designed to be a practical guide and a source of inspiration for anyone ready to embrace AI as a powerful ally in their productivity journey. As AI continues to evolve, learning how to effectively incorporate these tools can transform not only individual productivity but also the potential for success in an increasingly automated and digital world.

Chapter 1: Understanding AI and Its Role in Productivity

AI has quickly moved from being a futuristic concept to a powerful, everyday tool that impacts countless tasks in our personal and professional lives. To unlock AI's full potential for productivity, it's essential to understand some of the basic concepts and how they apply to real-life tasks. This chapter demystifies AI by explaining core concepts like machine learning, natural language processing (NLP), and predictive analytics, providing a solid foundation for understanding how AI-driven tools enhance efficiency, accuracy, and time management.

Demystifying AI for the Everyday User

For many, the term "artificial intelligence" can evoke images of highly complex systems and algorithms. In reality, AI refers to a set of technologies designed to mimic human intelligence and reasoning to accomplish specific tasks more efficiently. Let's break down three key components of AI:

1. **Machine Learning (ML):** This is the backbone of many AI tools, allowing systems to learn from data over time. Imagine a recommendation

algorithm on a streaming service: each time you watch something, the system "learns" more about your preferences, refining its suggestions. In the workplace, machine learning can help automate repetitive data-driven tasks, like sorting emails or analyzing sales patterns, by learning from past behaviors and patterns.

2. **Natural Language Processing (NLP):** NLP allows machines to understand, interpret, and generate human language. Chatbots and language models like ChatGPT use NLP to respond to questions and converse naturally with users. In daily work tasks, NLP-powered tools can summarize documents, help with translations, or assist in drafting emails, saving considerable time and effort.

3. **Predictive Analytics:** This concept involves using historical data to make forecasts. Predictive analytics can be seen in tools that, for instance, help sales teams by identifying which leads are most likely to convert based on past data. For marketers, it's a game-changer, as they can predict customer preferences, optimize campaigns, and improve targeting strategies.

The Productivity Potential of AI

AI-driven tools can improve productivity in the workplace by streamlining tasks, enhancing accuracy, and saving time, allowing people to focus on higher-value work. Imagine you're managing a project that requires a lot of routine, repetitive data entry. With an AI-powered automation tool, you could input data with minimal manual work, drastically reducing the risk of human error. Meanwhile, AI-driven scheduling tools can handle administrative work such as managing calendars or setting up meetings based on availability, helping professionals make the most of each day.

Beyond streamlining tasks, AI improves the quality of work. For instance, AI-powered grammar tools can ensure writing is clear, polished, and free of errors, whether for a quick email or an in-depth report. These tools don't just check grammar but also provide stylistic suggestions, making them useful for professionals and students alike. Another powerful AI application is in data analysis, where platforms can sort through vast amounts of data, identify trends, and present actionable insights in visual formats. This kind of analysis can be invaluable for business decision-making, whether in sales projections, risk assessments, or customer feedback analysis.

Popular AI Tools and Their Applications

AI tools are now available for various tasks, tailored to meet specific needs across diverse industries. Here's an overview of popular AI tools and their applications, categorized by purpose:

1. **Writing and Content Creation:**

    o **ChatGPT and Jasper** are AI-driven writing assistants that help generate content, brainstorm ideas, and even overcome writer's block. Professionals and content creators can save hours by using these tools to draft reports, emails, and articles.

- o **Grammarly and ProWritingAid** are used for editing and enhancing writing quality. They provide advanced grammar checks, readability scoring, and style suggestions, making them essential for students, writers, and business professionals.

2. **Creative Work:**

- o **DALL-E and Midjourney** are image-generation tools that use machine learning to create high-quality visuals. For designers and marketers, these tools are invaluable, producing unique images and graphics for social media, websites, and advertisements.

- o **Canva** incorporates AI features to simplify graphic design, allowing users without a design background to create professional visuals for presentations, marketing materials, and social media posts.

3. **Project Management and Workflow Optimization:**

- o **Trello, Asana, and Monday.com** use AI to enhance project tracking and team collaboration. These platforms can automate task assignments, send reminders, and even prioritize tasks based on urgency and deadlines, making team management more efficient.

- **Notion and ClickUp** combine project management with document creation, allowing teams to collaborate in real time, share notes, and organize tasks in one centralized platform.

4. **Task Automation and Data Handling:**

   - **Zapier and IFTTT** allow users to connect apps and automate workflows, performing repetitive tasks automatically. For instance, Zapier can sync data between applications or trigger emails when specific events occur, reducing manual effort.

   - **Tableau and Power BI** provide powerful data visualization capabilities, making it easier for businesses to interpret complex data and make informed decisions. By translating raw data into graphs and charts, they provide insights that are more actionable and easier to digest.

5. **Research and Knowledge Building:**

   - **Elicit and Scholarcy** help students and researchers by summarizing articles, generating citations, and even answering questions related to specific topics. These tools speed up the research process and support learning, especially when dealing with large amounts of academic content.

   - **LinkedIn Learning and Coursera** utilize AI to recommend courses and create personalized learning paths, making professional development accessible and targeted.

Understanding and implementing these AI tools can lead to immediate gains in productivity, freeing up time for more strategic, creative, and impactful work. Whether used for writing, data analysis, or task management, AI is reshaping how we work, allowing us to tackle tasks with greater speed and accuracy. Embracing these tools is less about replacing human effort and more about augmenting our capabilities, enabling everyone from students to seasoned professionals to unlock new levels of productivity. As we explore the vast landscape of AI tools throughout this guide, remember that the ultimate goal of these technologies is to help you work smarter, achieve more, and find balance in today's fast-paced work environment.

Chapter 2: Best AI Tools for Writing and Content Creation

The landscape of writing and content creation has seen a major shift with the introduction of AI tools, enabling faster content development and enhanced creative potential. Whether it's crafting a compelling blog post, developing narratives for novels, or refining professional reports, AI tools provide targeted support, helping writers overcome obstacles like writer's block, complex editing tasks, and research bottlenecks.

Here's a closer look at specific tools and how they impact different aspects of writing.

AI for Writing: Streamlining the Creative Process

For many, getting started is the hardest part of writing. AI tools like ChatGPT and Jasper facilitate the early stages of content creation by helping writers generate ideas, create outlines, and even draft content with minimal effort.

1. **ChatGPT:**

   o Idea Generation: ChatGPT can suggest themes, subtopics, and relevant points based on a simple prompt. For instance, if a writer is developing an article on "eco-friendly business practices," ChatGPT can quickly generate lists of sustainable practices, such as reducing waste, adopting renewable energy, and using biodegradable materials. This initial idea pool allows writers to start with clear angles and subtopics, saving hours of brainstorming.

- Draft Creation: By inputting a detailed outline, writers can use ChatGPT to generate entire paragraphs or sections of text. For example, a small business owner working on a blog post can use ChatGPT to draft different sections by specifying the tone (informative, persuasive, etc.), reducing the time it takes to produce a polished piece.

- Tailoring Responses with Custom Prompts: ChatGPT's responses become more refined with specific prompts. For example, when a writer needs information about the latest developments in AI, specifying a prompt like "Describe recent advancements in AI applications for education in layman's terms" can yield tailored insights, making it easier to reach non-technical audiences.

2. Jasper:

- Command Mode for Advanced Writing: Jasper's "Command" mode lets users provide detailed instructions to create content in specific formats, like listicles, FAQs, or summaries. A content creator tasked with generating multiple product descriptions for an e-commerce website can input a prompt like "Create a list of key features for a wireless Bluetooth speaker," and Jasper will produce succinct, high-impact copy suited for online marketing.

o Tone Adjustments and Keyword Integration: Jasper allows writers to specify the tone (e.g., conversational, formal) and insert keywords for SEO purposes, streamlining the process for digital marketers. Imagine a freelancer needing to write blog content optimized for search engines; they can input targeted keywords like "remote work tools" and "productivity hacks," allowing Jasper to generate SEO-friendly copy ready for publication.

Novel Writing with AI

AI also supports long-form content like novels, where writers require assistance in maintaining plot coherence, enhancing character development, and generating descriptive details. Sudowrite stands out as a specialized tool for creative fiction writing.

1. **Sudowrite:**

    ○ Descriptive Assistance: Sudowrite's "Describe" feature can help writers add depth and detail to scenes, providing suggestions for sensory elements like sight, sound, and smell. For example, a novelist describing a bustling marketplace scene might use Sudowrite to evoke a vivid picture, offering phrases about aromas of fresh spices, the chatter of vendors, and the warm sun casting golden light.

- Character Voice and Dialogue: Crafting authentic dialogue is challenging, especially in historical or genre-specific narratives. Sudowrite can generate context-appropriate dialogue, assisting a writer creating a 19th-century historical novel with expressions and vocabulary suited to the time period. This helps make dialogue feel more realistic and engaging.

- Plot Twist Generator: Sudowrite's "Twist" feature suggests unexpected plot turns. For a thriller writer struggling to maintain suspense, Sudowrite can propose plausible but surprising events that keep readers engaged, like a trusted character turning into an antagonist or a seemingly unrelated event that ties back into the main storyline.

Editing and Polishing Text

AI tools like Grammarly and ProWritingAid go beyond grammar correction, offering insights into style, clarity, and readability, which are invaluable for creating professional, polished text.

1. **Grammarly:**

   - Real-Time Suggestions for Grammar and Syntax: Grammarly's live suggestions enable writers to correct errors as they write. Imagine a business professional drafting a formal email: Grammarly's real-time feedback can correct any mistakes instantly, ensuring the email maintains professionalism.

- o Tone Detection: Grammarly identifies tone, which is helpful for adjusting content to suit different audiences. If a writer wants to adjust the tone of a press release from neutral to positive, Grammarly provides suggestions to make language more upbeat, enhancing the piece's engagement potential.

- o Readability Score and Suggestions: Grammarly's readability insights show whether the text is accessible or overly complex. For instance, a technical writer can use Grammarly to simplify jargon-heavy sections, making the content easier to read for a general audience.

2. **ProWritingAid:**

- o Comprehensive Reports on Style and Consistency: ProWritingAid generates reports on style, structure, pacing, and repetition, offering deeper insights than basic grammar checks. A novelist can use these reports to identify pacing issues in a manuscript, ensuring that the story flows at an engaging rhythm.

- o Contextual Thesaurus Suggestions: For more nuanced language use, ProWritingAid suggests alternative words based on context. A non-native English speaker writing an academic paper could rely on ProWritingAid to select sophisticated synonyms that elevate the paper's academic tone without misusing complex vocabulary.

- Visualization Tools for Sentence Structure: ProWritingAid offers graphs that break down sentence length and variation, helping writers create a rhythm that enhances readability. This feature is beneficial for scriptwriters who want to vary sentence lengths to create dynamic dialogue and maintain the audience's interest.

AI-Powered Tools for Students and Professionals

AI isn't just for writers—students and professionals who manage large volumes of information can benefit from research-focused AI tools like Elicit and Scholarcy.

1. **Elicit:**

    o Evidence-Based Summaries: Elicit scans academic literature to generate concise, evidence-based summaries. A graduate student working on a literature review can input research questions, and Elicit will return summaries from studies relevant to those questions, saving hours of manual review.

- Question-Driven Research: Elicit's Q&A function allows users to ask research-based questions and receive direct answers drawn from aggregated studies. This feature is especially useful for professionals in need of quick insights on topics like "effective remote work strategies" or "current market trends in sustainability."

- Source Comparison: Elicit can compare findings from multiple sources, giving a balanced view of complex topics. This is ideal for researchers or students who need a snapshot of varied perspectives in their field, like exploring the pros and cons of renewable energy.

2. **Scholarcy:**

- Automated Summary and Highlight Extraction: Scholarcy can generate summaries from research papers, breaking down complex arguments into digestible points. For example, a medical professional can use Scholarcy to review recent studies quickly, focusing on abstracts and key findings without getting lost in technical details.

- Automatic Citation Generation: Scholarcy extracts citations, saving students and researchers time when referencing sources. This feature is invaluable in academic writing, where managing dozens of sources can be tedious and time-consuming.

Encouragement to Explore and Customize Tools

While AI tools come with pre-set functions, personalizing them can enhance productivity significantly. Here's how users can take full advantage of customization options:

- Set Parameters Based on Goals: Adjust settings like tone, complexity, and output format. A freelance writer, for example, can tailor Jasper's outputs to match client-specific styles or audiences, producing tailored results that don't require extensive revisions.

- Experiment and Iterate with Prompts: Adjusting prompts or questions yields better results. For instance, a marketing professional using ChatGPT for ad copy might start with a broad prompt and refine it to include product benefits, target demographics, and preferred language style, ensuring that the output closely aligns with the campaign goals.

- Stay Open to New Features and Updates: AI tools constantly evolve, with regular updates bringing new functionalities. By exploring these updates, users can find novel ways to apply AI to their specific tasks, from generating interactive elements for digital content to synthesizing multimedia materials for educational purposes.

In Summary

AI tools like ChatGPT, Jasper, Grammarly, and ProWritingAid each offer unique advantages that cater to specific writing and research needs. By automating aspects of writing, editing, and research, these tools free users to focus on creative, strategic elements. Customizing and experimenting with these tools maximizes productivity, helping students, writers, and professionals alike achieve efficient, high-quality output.

Chapter 3: Visual Creativity with AI – Tools for Artists and Designers

The intersection of artificial intelligence and creative design is a dynamic frontier reshaping how artists and designers approach their craft. From generating stunning visuals to simplifying the design process, AI tools empower creators to enhance their work while preserving their unique artistic voices. Here's an in-depth look at the most impactful AI tools for visual creativity, practical applications, and tips for ensuring a balance between creativity and automation.

AI Tools for Creating Images and Graphics

The emergence of advanced AI tools like **DALL-E, Midjourney**, and **Canva's AI features** has revolutionized the way creators generate images and graphics, enabling them to produce high-quality visuals quickly and efficiently.

1. **DALL-E:**

    ○ **Image Generation from Text Prompts**: DALL-E, developed by OpenAI, allows users to create unique images by inputting descriptive text prompts. For instance, an interior designer could input a prompt like "a modern living room with mid-century furniture and indoor plants," generating an array of customized visuals that align with their design concept. This capability not only saves time but also encourages experimentation—designers can brainstorm ideas by seeing visual representations of concepts they may not have initially considered.

○ **Exploration of Artistic Styles**: Users can experiment with various artistic styles, asking DALL-E to create images in the style of famous artists or specific genres (e.g., surrealism, impressionism). A graphic novelist might input "a mystical forest in the style of Van Gogh," resulting in a vibrant and emotive background for their comic panels. This flexibility to explore diverse aesthetics encourages creativity and innovation, leading to unique storytelling elements.

○ **Collaboration and Iteration**: DALL-E allows for multiple iterations, so creators can refine their prompts based on initial outputs. A marketing team may generate several versions of a campaign image, iterating based on feedback until achieving the perfect representation of their brand message. This iterative process promotes a culture of continuous improvement, inviting artists to embrace experimentation as a vital component of their creative journey.

2. **Midjourney**:

   - **Community-Driven Image Creation**: Midjourney, primarily accessed through Discord, fosters a collaborative environment where users share prompts and results. An illustrator working on a graphic novel might share their generated images with fellow creators to gather feedback and inspiration. This community aspect allows artists to exchange ideas and find inspiration in others' creations, enhancing the collaborative spirit of the creative process.

   - **Fine-Tuning Capabilities**: Midjourney offers features for fine-tuning images through variations and adjustments. For example, a fashion designer can produce multiple versions of a clothing design, experimenting with colors and fabrics until they find the ideal combination that resonates with their audience. This flexibility encourages creators to push their boundaries and explore new possibilities, fostering a growth mindset that embraces change and innovation.

   - **Real-World Applications**: Artists and designers can use Midjourney for creating concept art for video games, visualizing characters and settings before diving into more detailed designs. A game designer might input a prompt for a "futuristic city skyline at sunset," quickly generating visuals that can guide the artistic direction of the game. This rapid prototyping helps in gaining client approval or showcasing ideas during pitch meetings.

3. **Canva's AI Tools**:

   o **User-Friendly Graphic Design**: Canva's AI-powered tools simplify graphic design for users at all skill levels. For instance, a local bakery owner looking to create eye-catching social media posts can use Canva's template library and AI-driven design suggestions to generate professional visuals showcasing their latest pastries. This accessibility democratizes design, allowing anyone to express their ideas visually, regardless of their technical skills.

   o **Background Remover and Image Enhancements**: Canva offers AI tools that enable users to easily remove backgrounds from images or enhance visuals with filters and adjustments. A photographer wanting to create a professional portfolio might use these features to curate their best work, ensuring each image looks polished and cohesive. The ability to enhance visual content effortlessly empowers users to produce high-quality materials that reflect their unique brand identity.

- ○ **Customizable Templates for Different Needs**: Canva provides a range of customizable templates that can save time when creating marketing materials. An online educator may adapt a webinar promotional template, quickly designing graphics that reflect their brand's aesthetics and engaging potential students. By encouraging users to personalize templates, Canva fosters a sense of ownership over the final product, enhancing user satisfaction and engagement.

Using AI for Book Covers and Marketing Materials

For authors and entrepreneurs, the visual appeal of marketing materials can significantly impact engagement and sales. AI-generated images can play a pivotal role in crafting compelling visuals for book covers and promotional content.

1. **Creating Eye-Catching Book Covers**:

    o   **Unique Design Elements**: Authors can use AI tools to generate unique artwork that reflects their book's themes. For instance, a science fiction author could input a prompt describing their book's futuristic setting, leading to a striking cover that captivates potential readers. By visualizing complex ideas through AI, authors can effectively communicate their stories' essence before the words are even read. This ability to generate personalized designs enhances the author's brand and elevates their work, making it more marketable.

- **Rapid Prototyping**: AI allows authors to quickly prototype multiple cover designs and select the one that resonates most with their target audience. For example, after generating different variations of a cover for a thriller novel, the author can conduct a poll among readers to see which design generates the most excitement. This process helps authors make data-driven decisions that ultimately lead to a more polished and appealing final product.

2. **Social Media and Advertisement Visuals**:

- **Consistent Branding**: Entrepreneurs can use AI-generated visuals to create cohesive branding across social media platforms. A skincare brand might generate a series of images featuring their products in different natural settings, maintaining a consistent aesthetic that enhances brand recognition. This strong visual identity fosters trust and loyalty among customers, reinforcing the importance of visual appeal in marketing.

- o **Promotional Graphics**: AI tools can streamline the creation of marketing materials, such as flyers, posters, and social media posts. A restaurant owner might generate promotional images of their signature dishes, quickly creating eye-catching content to share with their audience. This ease of creation empowers business owners to focus more on their core operations, knowing that high-quality visuals are just a few clicks away.

- o **A/B Testing for Marketing Campaigns**: AI-generated images can also facilitate A/B testing, allowing marketers to compare the performance of different visuals in advertisements. By analyzing engagement metrics, such as click-through rates and conversions, marketers can refine their campaigns to focus on the images that resonate best with their audience. For instance, a tech startup could run ads featuring two different visuals of their latest gadget, using performance data to identify which resonates more with potential customers.

Practical Tips for Balancing Creativity and Automation

While AI tools offer powerful advantages, it's essential for creators to maintain a personal touch in their work to ensure uniqueness and align with their branding. Here are practical tips to achieve this balance:

1. **Personalize AI Outputs**:

    ○ **Add Custom Elements**: After generating images with AI tools, consider adding hand-drawn elements or custom graphics. For example, a children's book illustrator might use AI to generate a whimsical landscape and then overlay their illustrations of characters to create a unique scene. This approach can help infuse personal style into the final design, making it feel more authentic. By integrating personal touches, creators can connect with their audience on a deeper level, conveying authenticity and individuality.

- o **Incorporate Brand Colors and Fonts**: When using AI tools, ensure that generated visuals align with your brand's colors and fonts. A fitness coach developing promotional content for their online classes should use colors and typography that match their existing branding to reinforce brand identity, helping audiences recognize their work instantly. A strong brand identity fosters trust and engagement, allowing creators to build lasting relationships with their audience.

2. **Iterate and Refine**:

- o **Use AI as a Starting Point**: Treat AI-generated outputs as a foundation to build upon rather than final products. An artist might use an AI-generated abstract piece as the backdrop for their painting, enhancing it with personal brush strokes and details. This iterative approach encourages artists to embrace a mindset of growth and exploration, continuously evolving their craft. By experimenting with

AI outputs, creators can discover new techniques and develop their artistic style.

- Experiment with Styles: Don't hesitate to use AI tools to experiment with various styles and formats. A wedding photographer may generate images in different aesthetics, such as vintage or modern, then select the style that resonates most with their artistic vision. Embracing experimentation allows creators to discover new avenues of expression, pushing the boundaries of their creativity.

3. Maintain Authenticity:

- Share the Creative Process: Engage your audience by sharing insights into your creative process, including how you use AI tools. For example, a graphic designer could document their workflow on social media, showing followers how they generate images with AI and then refine them. By documenting your journey, you foster a connection with your audience, emphasizing the human element behind your creations. This transparency builds trust and encourages engagement, as audiences appreciate the authenticity of the creative journey.

- Critically Evaluate AI Outputs: Not every AI-generated image will fit your vision perfectly. Be selective about what you choose to incorporate, ensuring that the final product reflects your personal standards of quality and creativity. For instance, an author might generate a variety of cover designs, choosing only those that truly resonate with their vision for the book. By maintaining high standards, creators can elevate their work and ensure it resonates deeply with their audience.

In Summary

As we stand at the crossroads of technology and creativity, AI tools offer unprecedented opportunities for artists and designers to enhance their work. By embracing these tools, creators can streamline their processes, explore new styles, and produce stunning visuals that capture their unique visions. The magic of creativity lies in its ability to adapt, evolve, and inspire. As you harness the power of AI in your artistic journey, remember to infuse your personality into your work, ensuring that each creation resonates with authenticity and passion. Together, let's celebrate the fusion of technology and creativity, unlocking endless possibilities for artistic expression and innovation.

Chapter 4: AI Tools for Boosting Workplace Efficiency

The integration of AI tools into workplace environments is no longer a luxury but a necessity for achieving optimal productivity. This chapter explores the transformative impact of AI in automating tasks, enhancing data analysis, optimizing project management, and simplifying daily operations.

Automating Repetitive Tasks

The automation of repetitive tasks is a significant game-changer in workplace efficiency. By leveraging tools like **Zapier**, **IFTTT**, and **Notion**, organizations can significantly reduce the time spent on mundane activities, allowing employees to engage in more value-added tasks.

1. **Zapier**:

    o **Real-World Automation Scenarios**: A sales team can use Zapier to connect their CRM (e.g., Salesforce) with their email platform (e.g., Mailchimp). Whenever a new lead is added to the

CRM, Zapier can automatically add that lead to a Mailchimp list for email marketing campaigns. This integration ensures no lead is overlooked, and the marketing team can effectively nurture leads without manual data entry.

- **Case Study**: Buffer, a social media management tool, utilized Zapier to integrate various workflows, leading to a 25% reduction in time spent on administrative tasks. This allowed their team to concentrate on developing new features and engaging with their user community, ultimately enhancing customer satisfaction.

2. **IFTTT (If This Then That):**

- **Examples of Cross-Platform Automation**: An HR department can set up IFTTT applets to automatically log employee attendance data in a Google Sheet when a team member checks in through a specific app. This automation streamlines record-keeping and reduces the risk of human error.

- **Smart Office Automation**: Employees working remotely can create IFTTT applets to adjust their home office environments. For instance, when the workday ends, an applet can be set to dim the lights and turn off smart devices, promoting energy conservation and signaling the end of the workday.

3. **Notion**:

   o **Customization and Workflow Creation**: Notion allows teams to build customized dashboards that reflect their unique workflows. A marketing team could create a content calendar template, complete with automated reminders for posting deadlines. When a content piece is due, team members receive notifications, ensuring timely execution of their marketing strategies.

   o **Integration with Other Tools**: Users can integrate Notion with tools like Google Calendar to automatically sync deadlines. This integration means that any change made in Notion automatically reflects in the Google Calendar, minimizing the risk of double booking or missed appointments.

Data Analysis and Reporting Tools

Data is the backbone of informed decision-making. Tools like **Tableau** and **MonkeyLearn** empower organizations to analyze large datasets quickly and efficiently, providing insights that drive strategy and innovation.

1. **Tableau**:

    o **Visualizing Complex Data Sets**: A healthcare organization could use Tableau to analyze patient data from various departments. By creating interactive dashboards, they can visualize patient wait times, treatment effectiveness, and resource allocation. This visualization enables quick identification of bottlenecks and informs strategies to improve patient care and operational efficiency.

- **Predictive Analytics**: Tableau can also incorporate predictive analytics to forecast future trends based on historical data. For example, a retail company can analyze purchasing patterns to predict seasonal demand, allowing them to optimize inventory levels and enhance supply chain management.

2. **MonkeyLearn**:

- **Text Analysis for Customer Insights**: A tech startup can utilize MonkeyLearn to analyze customer feedback from multiple platforms, such as social media, surveys, and reviews. By employing sentiment analysis, they can gauge customer satisfaction and identify common pain points. This data can then inform product development and marketing strategies.

- **Automating Report Generation**: MonkeyLearn can be set up to automatically generate reports on customer sentiment and feedback trends weekly. This automation ensures that stakeholders receive timely insights without the manual effort of collating and analyzing data.

Task Management and Workflow Optimization

Efficient project management is essential for team success. AI-enhanced platforms like **Trello**, **Asana**, and **Monday.com** provide robust features for tracking progress, managing tasks, and enhancing collaboration.

1. **Trello**:

   ○ **Customizable Workflow Automation**: Teams can create Trello boards tailored to specific projects, utilizing templates for consistent tracking. For example, a product launch team might have a board with lists for brainstorming, in-progress tasks, and completed tasks, facilitating clear visibility of project status.

- **Integration with Other Tools**: Trello integrates with Slack, allowing teams to receive notifications directly in their communication channels. For instance, when a card is moved to the "Completed" list, a message can automatically post in Slack, keeping everyone informed without needing to check Trello continuously.

2. **Asana**:

- **Dependency Management**: Asana allows teams to create task dependencies, ensuring that tasks are completed in the correct order. For example, in software development, a testing phase cannot start until development is complete. This feature prevents project delays and ensures streamlined workflows.

- **Workload Balancing**: Asana's reporting tools can provide insights into team member workloads, highlighting who may be overburdened and who has capacity for additional tasks. A project manager can then redistribute assignments based on these insights, promoting a balanced workload and reducing burnout.

3. **Monday.com:**

- **Visual Project Tracking**: Monday.com offers a visual approach to project management with its Kanban-style boards. A marketing team can visualize their campaigns' timelines, deadlines, and responsibilities, ensuring everyone is aligned on objectives and progress.

- **Collaboration Features**: Teams can leave comments and attach files directly on tasks, centralizing communication within the platform. This feature reduces email clutter and ensures that all project-related discussions are accessible and organized.

AI Assistants for Everyday Tasks

AI virtual assistants like **Google Assistant** and **Siri** play a pivotal role in enhancing productivity by streamlining daily tasks and providing valuable support.

1. **Google Assistant**:

    o **Hands-Free Management**: Google Assistant can manage daily schedules, allowing users to add calendar events or reminders through voice commands. For instance, a project manager might say, "Hey Google, remind me to review the budget report at 2 PM," ensuring that critical tasks are not forgotten.

- **Integration with Smart Devices**: In a hybrid work environment, Google Assistant can help manage smart office devices, such as adjusting lighting and temperature settings during working hours. This capability enhances comfort and productivity, particularly for those working from home.

2. Siri:

- **Streamlining Communication**: Siri can send messages or make calls, helping users maintain communication without interrupting their workflow. For example, a team leader can dictate a quick message to a colleague while preparing for a meeting, ensuring that important communications occur swiftly.

- **Setting Contextual Reminders**: Siri can set reminders based on context, such as location. A sales rep could say, "Remind me to send the follow-up email when I get to the office," ensuring that important tasks are completed promptly.

Conclusion

Incorporating AI tools into workplace operations presents a powerful opportunity for organizations to enhance efficiency, streamline workflows, and drive productivity. By automating repetitive tasks, leveraging advanced data analysis, optimizing project management, and utilizing virtual assistants for daily tasks, businesses can focus on strategic initiatives that lead to growth and success. As AI continues to evolve, its role in the workplace will only become more integral, allowing organizations to remain competitive in an increasingly fast-paced business landscape.

Industry-Specific Applications of AI Tools

Exploring how AI tools are tailored for specific industries can provide valuable insights into their effectiveness and relevance. Here are a few key industries that benefit significantly from AI-driven productivity tools:

1. **Healthcare:**

   o **Patient Management Systems**: AI tools like **Epic** use predictive analytics to forecast patient admissions, optimize staffing, and manage resources efficiently. This enables healthcare providers to enhance patient care while reducing operational costs.

   o **Telemedicine Integration**: AI-driven platforms, such as **Zocdoc**, streamline the appointment scheduling process for patients. By using machine learning algorithms, these tools can match patients with the right healthcare providers based on their needs and preferences, making healthcare more accessible.

2. **Finance:**

   o **Automated Financial Analysis**: Tools like **Kabbage** utilize AI to analyze business cash flow and provide instant loan approvals. This reduces the time spent on manual reviews and accelerates funding for small businesses.

- o **Fraud Detection**: Financial institutions employ AI-driven systems such as **Darktrace** to monitor transactions and detect unusual patterns indicative of fraud. This proactive approach helps safeguard assets and maintain customer trust.

3. **Manufacturing**:

- o **Predictive Maintenance**: AI tools like **Uptake** analyze machine performance data to predict maintenance needs before failures occur. This reduces downtime and extends the lifespan of equipment, ultimately leading to cost savings.

- o **Supply Chain Optimization**: Companies like **IBM** use AI to enhance supply chain management by forecasting demand and optimizing inventory levels. This ensures that manufacturers can meet customer demands without overproducing, thus minimizing waste.

4. **Education**:

- o **Personalized Learning Platforms**: AI tools such as **Knewton** provide personalized learning experiences by adapting content based on individual student performance and learning styles. This tailored approach enhances student engagement and achievement.

○ **Automated Grading Systems**: Tools like **Gradescope** utilize AI to assist educators in grading assignments more efficiently. By automating the grading of multiple-choice and short-answer questions, teachers can dedicate more time to providing personalized feedback.

Human-AI Collaboration in the Workplace

As AI tools become more integrated into daily workflows, the concept of human-AI collaboration emerges as a crucial theme. Rather than replacing human roles, AI enhances human capabilities, leading to more effective teamwork and innovative problem-solving.

1. **Augmented Decision-Making**:

   ○ **Real-Time Insights**: AI tools can analyze data and present insights in real-time, allowing employees to make informed decisions quickly. For instance, a marketing manager using **HubSpot** can leverage AI analytics to determine the most effective campaign strategies based on live consumer behavior data.

   ○ **Scenario Planning**: By utilizing AI-driven forecasting tools, businesses can simulate various scenarios based on changing market conditions. This capability empowers teams to explore potential outcomes and develop strategic responses.

2. **Enhanced Creativity**:

   o **Collaborative Brainstorming**: AI tools like **Miro** can facilitate collaborative brainstorming sessions, allowing team members to contribute ideas in real-time. The AI can then analyze these ideas, categorizing them and suggesting the most promising concepts to pursue.

   o **Content Generation**: While AI can generate content, it can also serve as a collaborative partner in the creative process. For example, writers can use tools like **ChatGPT** to explore different narrative angles, enhancing the richness of their storytelling.

3. **Training and Development**:

   o **Skill Assessment**: AI tools can evaluate employee skills and recommend personalized development paths. For instance, platforms like **Degreed** use AI to analyze employee performance and suggest relevant courses to fill skill gaps.

   o **Continuous Learning**: AI can curate personalized learning materials, adapting to employees' changing needs and helping them stay current in their fields.

This promotes a culture of continuous improvement and adaptability.

The Future of AI in Workplace Efficiency

Looking ahead, the potential for AI to transform workplace efficiency continues to grow. Here are some emerging trends and concepts shaping the future landscape of AI in the workplace:

1. **AI-Driven Decision Support Systems:**

   o Future workplace environments may see more sophisticated decision support systems powered by AI. These systems could analyze historical and real-time data to provide recommendations, helping leaders navigate complex decisions with confidence.

2. **Increased Personalization:**

   o As AI technologies evolve, the ability to personalize tools and experiences will enhance. For instance, AI-driven HR platforms might offer tailored career development paths based on individual employee aspirations and performance metrics.

3. **Ethical AI and Accountability:**

   o As AI becomes more prevalent, the conversation around ethical AI practices will intensify. Companies will need to prioritize transparency and accountability in their AI systems, ensuring that algorithms are fair and that employee privacy is protected.

4. **Hybrid Work Models:**

   - The rise of hybrid work models necessitates AI solutions that can seamlessly support both in-office and remote employees. Tools that facilitate collaboration, project management, and communication will be crucial in maintaining productivity in this new work paradigm.

Conclusion

AI's role in boosting workplace efficiency is multifaceted, touching every aspect of business operations. By embracing AI tools tailored for specific industries, fostering human-AI collaboration, and anticipating future trends, organizations can not only enhance their productivity but also create a dynamic and adaptive work environment. As we continue to explore and innovate with AI, the possibilities for improving efficiency and achieving success in the modern workplace are limitless.

Chapter 5: Elevating Learning and Professional Growth with AI

In today's fast-paced world, the ability to learn and adapt quickly is essential for personal and professional success. AI-powered tools are transforming the landscape of education and skill development, providing tailored solutions that enhance learning experiences and professional growth. This chapter explores how these tools empower students, professionals, and lifelong learners to achieve their goals.

AI-Powered Research Tools for Students and Researchers

The digital age has made information more accessible than ever, but sifting through vast amounts of data can be overwhelming. AI-powered research tools are designed to help students and researchers streamline their work, saving time and improving the quality of their output.

1. **ChatGPT for Research Assistance**:
    - ○ ChatGPT, a conversational AI tool, is revolutionizing the way students approach research. It can assist in formulating research questions, generating outlines,

and summarizing complex articles. For example, a university student researching climate change can ask ChatGPT for a summary of recent studies, allowing them to grasp essential findings without getting bogged down in extensive reading.

- Furthermore, ChatGPT can generate study guides based on specific topics. Students can input their lecture notes, and the AI can help create concise study materials, making exam preparation more efficient.

2. **Perplexity for Information Discovery**:

- Perplexity is an AI-powered search engine that provides instant answers and summarizes sources in real time. For instance, a researcher investigating renewable energy technologies can input questions and receive well-sourced responses, complete with citations, enhancing the credibility of their work.

- This tool is particularly beneficial for academic writing, where proper citations are crucial. By using Perplexity, students can ensure they accurately reference their sources, saving time on the research process while maintaining academic integrity.

Developing New Skills Through AI-Powered Platforms

The need for continuous skill development has never been more pronounced, and AI is at the forefront of personalizing the learning experience.

1. **LinkedIn Learning**:
   - LinkedIn Learning employs AI algorithms to recommend courses based on users' current skills, career goals, and industry trends. For example, a marketing professional looking to expand their digital marketing skills might be suggested courses on SEO, content strategy, and

analytics, all tailored to their interests and professional trajectory.

- o The platform tracks progress and adjusts recommendations dynamically, ensuring that learners are always challenged but not overwhelmed. This tailored approach helps professionals upskill efficiently, making them more competitive in the job market.

2. **Coursera's Adaptive Learning Paths**:

- o Coursera uses AI to create adaptive learning paths for users based on their prior knowledge and learning pace. For instance, someone interested in data science can take a skills assessment, and the platform will customize their course recommendations, suggesting beginner courses in statistics and programming before advancing to more complex topics like machine learning.

- o This personalization fosters a deeper understanding of the material, as learners are guided through a structured path that builds their knowledge incrementally, rather than feeling lost in a sea of content.

AI Tools for Skill Enhancement in Specific Fields

AI is also reshaping the way individuals acquire specialized skills tailored to specific professions.

1. **Duolingo for Language Learning**:

   o Duolingo has transformed language acquisition with its gamified, AI-driven approach. The platform adapts lessons based on users' strengths and weaknesses, offering targeted exercises to reinforce areas that need improvement. For example, if a user struggles with verb conjugation in Spanish, Duolingo will provide additional practice focused on that topic, ensuring a more effective learning experience.

○ The app also uses AI to predict when learners are likely to forget material and sends timely reminders for practice, enhancing long-term retention.

2. **DeepL for Professional Translation**:

○ For professionals needing translation services, DeepL employs advanced AI to provide high-quality translations that often surpass traditional translation tools. This is particularly beneficial in industries like legal, medical, or technical fields, where accuracy is critical. A legal professional might use DeepL to translate documents while ensuring that nuanced legal terms are appropriately interpreted.

○ Moreover, DeepL's interface allows users to edit translations in real-time, providing instant feedback and helping users learn from mistakes. This interactivity empowers users to develop their language skills alongside their translation needs.

Conclusion: Embracing AI for Lifelong Learning

The integration of AI into learning and professional development is not just a trend; it's a transformative shift that enhances accessibility, personalization, and efficiency. By leveraging AI-powered tools, students and professionals can navigate their educational journeys with greater confidence and effectiveness. As the landscape of work and education continues to evolve, embracing AI will be essential for those looking to thrive in their careers and beyond.

Incorporating these tools into everyday practice not only aids in skill acquisition but also fosters a mindset of lifelong learning—a vital asset in an ever-changing job market. As we look to the future, the potential for AI to enhance learning and professional growth remains vast, promising a world where everyone has the opportunity to reach their fullest potential.

AI has made significant inroads in fields like mathematics, physics, and engineering, enhancing both research and practical applications. Here's a deeper exploration of specific areas where AI is making a substantial impact in these disciplines:

1. Mathematics

Automated Theorem Proving

AI systems are being developed to automate the process of proving mathematical theorems. For instance, tools like **Lean** and **Coq** allow mathematicians to formalize proofs and check their correctness automatically. This has the potential to reduce errors in complex proofs and enable mathematicians to explore new areas of research more efficiently.

Data-Driven Modeling

In applied mathematics, AI can help build predictive models based on historical data. For example, using **machine learning algorithms** to analyze large datasets can identify patterns that traditional mathematical methods may miss. In climate modeling, AI can enhance the accuracy of predictive models for weather patterns by processing vast amounts of meteorological data.

Symbolic Mathematics

Tools like **SymPy** and **Mathematica** utilize AI to perform symbolic computation, allowing users to manipulate algebraic expressions analytically. This is particularly useful in educational settings, where students can receive instant feedback on their algebraic manipulations, helping them understand complex concepts more thoroughly.

2. Physics

Quantum Computing

AI is playing a critical role in the development of quantum computing. Algorithms like **Variational Quantum Eigensolver (VQE)** utilize machine learning to optimize quantum circuits, which can lead to breakthroughs in simulating quantum systems. This can help physicists solve problems related to quantum mechanics more efficiently, potentially leading to new materials and technologies.

Astrophysics and Cosmology

AI algorithms are increasingly used in analyzing astronomical data. For example, projects like the **Event**

Horizon Telescope used AI to reconstruct images of black holes from complex datasets. AI helps in identifying patterns in the data collected from telescopes, which can lead to discoveries of new celestial bodies or phenomena.

Particle Physics

In high-energy physics experiments, like those conducted at the **Large Hadron Collider (LHC)**, AI is employed to sift through enormous amounts of collision data. Techniques such as **deep learning** are used to identify rare particle events, helping physicists understand fundamental particles and forces better.

3. Engineering

Design Optimization

In engineering design, AI tools can optimize designs by evaluating countless iterations based on performance criteria. Software like **ANSYS** uses AI-driven algorithms to simulate and optimize product designs, such as in aerospace engineering, where weight reduction and aerodynamic efficiency are critical.

Predictive Maintenance

AI applications in engineering include predictive maintenance, where machine learning algorithms analyze data from sensors in machinery to predict failures before they occur. For instance, **General Electric** employs AI to monitor the health of jet engines, enabling timely maintenance and reducing downtime.

Structural Engineering

AI models can analyze structural integrity using data from sensors embedded in buildings or bridges. For instance, **IBM's Watson** has been applied to monitor the health of infrastructure, predicting potential issues and suggesting maintenance before catastrophic failures occur.

Robotics and Automation

AI has transformed engineering through advancements in robotics and automation. In manufacturing, AI-driven robots can adapt to changes in production lines, improving efficiency. For instance, **Fanuc's robots** use AI to learn from their environment, allowing them to handle complex tasks like assembly or packaging.

4. Education and Research Enhancement

Personalized Learning

In mathematics and physics education, AI-powered platforms like **Khan Academy** use algorithms to adapt to individual student needs, providing personalized resources and problems based on their performance. This ensures that students receive targeted assistance in areas where they struggle, ultimately improving learning outcomes.

Research Collaboration

AI facilitates collaboration among researchers by analyzing literature and suggesting relevant papers, researchers, or projects. Tools like **ResearchGate** leverage AI to connect scientists based on their research interests and publications, fostering collaboration across disciplines and geographical boundaries.

Conclusion: Embracing AI in STEM Fields

The integration of AI in mathematics, physics, and engineering is not just a trend; it is a fundamental shift that enhances research, education, and practical applications. By leveraging AI tools, professionals in these fields can achieve greater efficiency, uncover new insights, and innovate in ways previously thought impossible.

As these technologies continue to evolve, they promise to reshape the landscape of STEM disciplines, opening new frontiers for exploration and discovery. Whether through automating complex calculations, optimizing designs, or enhancing educational experiences, the potential of AI to revolutionize how we approach mathematics, physics, and engineering is immense.

Chapter 6: Addressing Ethical and Privacy Considerations in AI Use

In our increasingly digital and interconnected world, the adoption of artificial intelligence (AI) technologies presents not only tremendous opportunities for productivity and efficiency but also significant ethical and privacy challenges. As businesses and individuals harness AI to drive innovation and streamline operations, it is crucial to navigate the ethical landscape surrounding these powerful tools. This chapter explores key privacy concerns, the relevance of ethics in AI, and practical tips for ensuring responsible AI usage that aligns with personal and professional values.

Understanding Data Privacy and AI

One of the foremost concerns in the realm of AI is data privacy. AI systems rely heavily on vast amounts of data to learn and make decisions, often involving sensitive personal information. For instance, AI algorithms used in recruitment tools analyze candidates' resumes, social media activity, and even online behaviors to determine suitability for a job. This practice raises critical questions about the ownership of data, consent, and how that data is used.

- **Key Privacy Concerns**:

    - **Informed Consent**: Users must be informed about what data is being collected and how it will be used. For example, many health apps that utilize AI for fitness tracking ask for consent but may not clearly explain how the data will be stored or shared.

- ○ **Data Breaches**: As companies collect and store large volumes of personal data, they become attractive targets for cyberattacks. A breach can expose sensitive information, leading to identity theft or privacy violations. For example, the 2017 Equifax breach compromised the personal data of millions of individuals, highlighting the importance of robust data protection measures.

- ○ **Anonymization vs. Re-identification**: While organizations often anonymize data to protect individual identities, sophisticated algorithms can sometimes re-identify users. For instance, data originally stripped of personal identifiers can be cross-referenced with other datasets, potentially exposing private information.

Ethical AI and Its Relevance in the Workplace

As organizations implement AI tools, understanding ethical implications becomes imperative. Ethical AI refers to the principles that guide the design, development, and deployment of AI systems to ensure they are fair, transparent, and accountable.

- **Why Ethics Are Crucial**:

    - **Bias and Fairness**: AI systems can inadvertently perpetuate biases present in training data, leading to unfair outcomes. For example, facial recognition technology has been criticized for racial and gender biases, resulting in disproportionate misidentifications of individuals from minority groups. Companies like **IBM** are actively working on bias detection tools to mitigate these issues.

- **Transparency**: Users should understand how AI systems make decisions. For instance, if a bank uses AI to approve loans, applicants deserve transparency about the criteria used in the decision-making process. Initiatives like **Explainable AI (XAI)** aim to create models that are interpretable and understandable by humans.

- **Accountability**: Organizations must establish clear accountability mechanisms for AI-generated decisions. In scenarios where AI systems make errors, there should be processes to address grievances and rectify mistakes. For example, the **European Union's AI Act** seeks to hold companies accountable for AI systems that pose high risks to safety and fundamental rights.

Balancing Productivity with Integrity

As AI tools become integral to business processes, finding a balance between maximizing productivity and maintaining ethical standards is essential.

- **Practical Tips for Making AI an Ally**:

    - **Establish Clear Guidelines**: Organizations should develop and communicate ethical guidelines for AI usage that emphasize responsible data handling, bias mitigation, and transparency. Regular training sessions can help employees understand the implications of their AI-related decisions.

- Conduct Regular Audits: Regular audits of AI systems can help identify potential biases or ethical concerns. For instance, companies can conduct impact assessments to evaluate how their AI tools affect different demographics, ensuring equitable outcomes.

- Encourage Open Dialogue: Foster a culture of openness where employees can voice concerns about AI tools without fear of reprisal. Establishing ethics committees that include diverse perspectives can provide valuable insights into the ethical implications of AI initiatives.

- Integrate Human Oversight: While AI can automate many tasks, human oversight is crucial to maintain ethical standards. For instance, in hiring processes where AI tools are used, final decisions should involve human review to ensure fairness and accuracy.

Conclusion: Navigating the Ethical Landscape

As AI continues to transform the modern workplace, the ethical and privacy considerations surrounding its use cannot be overlooked. By understanding data privacy concerns, embracing ethical principles, and finding ways to align AI with personal and organizational values, individuals and businesses can leverage AI responsibly. This not only enhances productivity but also fosters trust and integrity in the workplace, ultimately leading to sustainable success.

Embracing ethical AI is not just a regulatory necessity; it is a moral imperative that shapes the future of work. By prioritizing responsible AI use, organizations can position themselves as leaders in an era where technology and ethics coexist harmoniously.

Here are some real-world case studies of companies that have successfully implemented AI tools in their workflows, showcasing specific outcomes like increased efficiency, cost savings, and improved employee satisfaction:

1. IBM – AI in Customer Service

Implementation: IBM introduced Watson, its AI platform, to enhance customer service for businesses. Watson uses natural language processing and machine learning to analyze customer queries and provide accurate responses.

Outcomes:

- **Increased Efficiency**: By automating routine customer inquiries, companies using Watson reduced response times significantly. For example, a major telecom provider saw a 50% reduction in customer service wait times.

- **Cost Savings**: The automation allowed companies to redirect customer service representatives to more complex issues, effectively reducing operational costs. One client reported a 20% decrease in customer service operational expenses.

- **Improved Employee Satisfaction**: With AI handling repetitive tasks, employees reported higher job satisfaction as they could focus on more engaging and challenging work.

2. Amazon – AI in Supply Chain and Logistics

Implementation: Amazon employs AI and machine learning algorithms to optimize its supply chain and logistics operations, including inventory management and delivery processes.

Outcomes:

- **Increased Efficiency**: AI algorithms analyze purchasing patterns and predict demand, allowing Amazon to optimize inventory levels. This has led to a 20% increase in inventory turnover rates.

- **Cost Savings**: Automated fulfillment centers equipped with AI technology have reduced labor costs and increased throughput, resulting in substantial savings. Amazon reported a 30% decrease in fulfillment costs over a three-year period.

- **Enhanced Customer Experience**: Faster and more accurate order processing has led to higher customer satisfaction, with positive reviews increasing by 15%.

3. Salesforce – AI in Sales and Marketing

Implementation: Salesforce integrated its AI tool, Einstein, into its Customer Relationship Management (CRM) platform. Einstein analyzes customer data to provide insights and recommendations for sales and marketing teams.

Outcomes:

- **Increased Efficiency**: Sales teams using Einstein reported a 25% increase in lead conversion rates as the tool helped prioritize high-value leads based on predictive analytics.

- **Cost Savings**: By automating routine data entry and analysis tasks, companies reduced the time sales representatives spent on administrative work by 30%, allowing them to focus more on closing deals.

- **Improved Employee Satisfaction**: Sales teams felt empowered by the insights provided by AI, which increased confidence in their strategies and enhanced overall job satisfaction.

4. Netflix – AI in Content Recommendation

Implementation: Netflix utilizes advanced algorithms to analyze user behavior and preferences to recommend content, enhancing the user experience.

Outcomes:

- **Increased Efficiency**: The recommendation system accounts for over 80% of the content watched on the platform, streamlining user engagement and making content discovery more efficient.

- **Cost Savings**: By using AI to personalize recommendations, Netflix minimizes the need for extensive marketing campaigns to promote content. This has resulted in significant cost savings, allowing for reinvestment into original content production.

- **Improved Customer Satisfaction**: The tailored experience has contributed to a rise in subscriber retention rates, with Netflix reporting a 93% customer satisfaction score due to personalized content recommendations.

5. General Electric (GE) – AI in Predictive Maintenance

Implementation: GE has implemented AI-driven predictive maintenance tools for its manufacturing equipment. These tools analyze data from machinery to predict potential failures before they occur.

Outcomes:

- **Increased Efficiency**: By predicting when maintenance is needed, GE reduced unplanned downtime by 20%, leading to smoother operations and increased productivity.

- **Cost Savings**: Predictive maintenance has resulted in a 10% reduction in maintenance costs, as issues can be addressed proactively rather than reactively.

- **Enhanced Employee Satisfaction**: Employees have expressed greater job satisfaction due to reduced stress and workload associated with unexpected equipment failures.

6. Zebra Technologies – AI in Inventory Management

Implementation: Zebra Technologies uses AI and machine learning in its inventory management systems to optimize stock levels and track product movement.

Outcomes:

- **Increased Efficiency**: Companies using Zebra's AI-driven inventory solutions reported a 30% reduction in stock discrepancies and a 25% improvement in order fulfillment times.

- **Cost Savings**: Improved inventory accuracy has led to decreased holding costs and reduced waste, resulting in savings of up to 20% in inventory management expenses.

- **Improved Employee Satisfaction**: Workers appreciated the reduction in manual counting and stock management tasks, allowing them to focus on more strategic responsibilities.

Conclusion

These case studies illustrate the diverse applications of AI across industries and highlight the tangible benefits that companies have experienced. By leveraging AI tools, organizations have been able to enhance productivity, reduce costs, and improve employee satisfaction, demonstrating the transformative power of AI in the modern workplace. As businesses continue to explore and implement AI technologies, they can expect to see further innovations and efficiencies that drive success.

Here's a step-by-step implementation guide for integrating AI tools into workflows, complete with practical steps for evaluation, selection, and training:

Step-by-Step Implementation Guide for Integrating AI Tools into Workflows

Step 1: Evaluate Your Needs

1. **Identify Pain Points:**

   - Conduct a thorough assessment of your current workflows.
   - Identify repetitive tasks, bottlenecks, or areas lacking efficiency.

2. **Define Goals:**

   - Determine what you aim to achieve with AI integration. Common goals include:
     - Increasing productivity
     - Reducing operational costs
     - Improving accuracy in data handling
     - Enhancing customer satisfaction

3. **Gather Stakeholder Input:**

   - Engage team members across various departments to gather insights on challenges they face and potential AI applications.

Step 2: Research and Select the Right AI Tools

1. **Explore Available Tools**:

   - Investigate different AI tools tailored to your identified needs. Key categories to explore include:

     - **Task Automation**: Tools like Zapier or IFTTT for streamlining repetitive tasks.

     - **Data Analysis**: Tools like Tableau or Microsoft Power BI for data visualization.

     - **Content Creation**: Tools like ChatGPT or Grammarly for writing assistance.

2. **Compare Features**:

   - Create a comparison matrix for the tools you're considering. Look at:

     - Features offered

     - Integration capabilities with existing systems

     - Scalability for future needs

     - User-friendliness

3. **Read Reviews and Case Studies**:

- Look for user reviews, case studies, or testimonials to understand how others have successfully implemented the tools.

4. **Trial and Testing**:

   - Take advantage of free trials or demo versions of the selected tools.

   - Involve a small group of users to test functionality and gather feedback.

Step 3: Plan the Integration Process

1. **Develop an Integration Plan**:

   - Outline a clear timeline and milestones for integration.

   - Specify which teams or departments will use each tool.

2. **Ensure Data Compatibility**:

   - Assess your existing data sources and ensure they can integrate smoothly with the new AI tools. This may require data cleaning or migration.

3. **Establish Support Structures**:

   - Designate team members or a task force to oversee the integration process and serve as points of contact for troubleshooting.

Step 4: Train Employees

1. **Create Training Programs**:

   - Develop training sessions tailored to different user levels (beginners, intermediate, advanced).

   - Consider various formats such as in-person workshops, online tutorials, or recorded webinars.

2. **Utilize Resources**:

   - Make use of available resources from the AI tool providers, such as user manuals, online courses, and community forums.

3. **Encourage Hands-On Practice**:

   - Provide opportunities for employees to experiment with the tools in a safe environment, such as through sandbox environments or test projects.

4. **Solicit Feedback**:

   - After training sessions, gather feedback from participants to improve future training and address any lingering uncertainties.

Step 5: Monitor and Adjust

1. **Set Metrics for Success**:

   - Define key performance indicators (KPIs) to measure the effectiveness of the AI tools. Examples include:

- Time saved on specific tasks

- Reduction in error rates

- Increased employee satisfaction scores

2. **Regular Check-Ins:**

   o Schedule regular meetings to assess the integration progress and gather feedback from users.

   o Use this feedback to make necessary adjustments to workflows or provide additional training.

3. **Stay Updated:**

   o Keep abreast of updates or new features released by the AI tool providers, as well as emerging tools that may further enhance productivity.

4. **Encourage a Culture of Continuous Improvement:**

   o Promote an organizational culture that values innovation and encourages team members to share insights and best practices regarding AI tool usage.

Conclusion

By following these steps, organizations can systematically integrate AI tools into their workflows, enhancing efficiency and productivity. The key is to remain adaptable, continuously evaluate the impact of the tools, and ensure that employees are well-equipped and supported throughout the transition.

Here's a comparison chart that outlines the features, benefits, and potential drawbacks of popular AI tools across various categories, including writing, project management, and design. This chart can help readers make informed decisions based on their specific needs.

Category	Tool	Key Features	Benefits	Potential Drawbacks
Writing	ChatGPT	- Natural language generation - Contextual understanding - Customizable prompts	- Generates creative content - Quick responses - Assists with brainstorming	- May produce inaccurate information - Requires careful editing
	Grammarly	- Grammar and style checking - Plagiarism detection - Tone suggestions	- Improves writing clarity - Enhances professionalism - User-friendly interface	- Premium features can be expensive - Limited functionality without internet
	Jasper	- AI content generation - SEO optimization tools	- Great for marketers - Saves time on content creation	- Learning curve for advanced features - Subscripti

Category	Tool	Key Features	Benefits	Potential Drawbacks
		- Templates for various content types	- Easy to use	on cost can add up
Project Management	Trello	- Visual task management - Custom boards and lists - Integration with other tools	- Simple interface - Flexible organization - Great for team collaboration	- Limited reporting capabilities - May require additional tools for full functionality
	Asana	- Task assignments - Timeline view - Reporting and analytics	- Comprehensive project tracking - Encourages accountability - Integrates well with other tools	- Can be overwhelming for new users - Some features are locked behind premium plans
	Monday.com	- Customizable workflows - Visual dashboards -	- Highly adaptable to various industries - Easy to track progress - Good	- Higher learning curve - Costs can increase with more users and

Category	Tool	Key Features	Benefits	Potential Drawbacks
		Automation capabilities	collaboration features	features
Design	Canva	- Drag-and-drop interface - Extensive template library - AI-powered design suggestions	- User-friendly for non-designers - Quick creation of marketing materials - Collaboration features	- Limited customization options for advanced users - Some premium assets require payment
	DALL-E	- AI image generation from text prompts - Customization options for styles and formats	- Generates unique visuals - Great for creative projects - Quick output	- Limited control over specific image details - May produce unpredictable results
	Midjourney	- High-quality image generation - Focus on artistic styles - Communit	- Unique art styles - Good for creative brainstorming - Engaging community	- Requires Discord access - Learning curve to master prompts

Category	Tool	Key Features	Benefits	Potential Drawbacks
		y-driven platform		
Research	Elicit	- Research summaries - Citation generation - Collaborative tools	- Streamlines literature reviews - Saves time on research - Easy to use	- May not cover all sources - Limited to specific research types
	Scholarcy	- Summarizes articles and papers - Creates flashcards - Reference extraction	- Helps digest complex material quickly - Good for studying - Supports various document types	- Accuracy can vary - Some features require subscription

Conclusion

This comparison chart provides a snapshot of the key features, benefits, and drawbacks of various AI tools across different categories. By evaluating these aspects, readers can make informed decisions about which tools best suit their needs and how to integrate them into their workflows for enhanced productivity and success.

Here's a discussion on **Future Trends in AI** that could significantly impact productivity in various sectors, highlighting the rise of generative AI, advancements in natural language processing (NLP), and the potential of AI in enhancing remote work.

Future Trends in AI Impacting Productivity

1. The Rise of Generative AI

Generative AI, which refers to algorithms capable of creating new content, is rapidly evolving and transforming numerous industries. As tools like ChatGPT and DALL-E become more sophisticated, their applications are broadening:

- **Content Creation**: Generative AI is revolutionizing content production by enabling faster generation of articles, marketing copy, social media posts, and more. Businesses can leverage these tools to produce high-quality content at scale, significantly reducing the time and costs associated with traditional writing processes.

- **Creative Arts**: Artists and designers are using generative AI to inspire new designs, music, and other artistic forms. This trend allows for unique collaborations between human creativity and machine learning, resulting in innovative works that push the boundaries of conventional art.

2. Advancements in Natural Language Processing (NLP)

NLP continues to improve, making AI systems more effective at understanding and generating human language. This advancement will have several implications:

- **Enhanced Communication**: Businesses can expect more advanced chatbots and virtual assistants that understand context better and can handle more complex queries. This improvement will lead to enhanced customer service experiences and streamlined internal communications.

- **Real-time Translation**: With advancements in NLP, real-time language translation will become more accessible, enabling global teams to collaborate more effectively. This capability will break down language barriers, fostering greater inclusivity and diversity in the workplace.

3. AI in Enhancing Remote Work

The COVID-19 pandemic has permanently shifted many organizations toward remote work. AI is playing a crucial role in optimizing this work model:

- **Productivity Monitoring Tools**: AI tools that track productivity and time management are becoming more sophisticated. They can analyze work patterns, providing insights that help employees optimize their schedules and enhance their focus on important tasks.

- **Virtual Collaboration**: AI is enhancing remote collaboration tools, making virtual meetings more productive. Features like automatic transcription, real-time language translation, and AI-driven agenda setting will help remote teams work more effectively and stay aligned.

4. Personalized Learning and Development

AI's capabilities in data analysis and pattern recognition are transforming employee training and development:

- **Tailored Learning Experiences**: AI can analyze employees' skills, preferences, and performance metrics to create personalized learning paths. This trend will lead to more effective training programs that address individual needs, helping employees acquire new skills relevant to their roles.

- **Continuous Feedback Mechanisms**: The integration of AI in learning platforms can provide continuous feedback and assessments, allowing employees to track their progress in real-time. This capability will foster a culture of continuous improvement and professional growth.

5. AI Ethics and Responsibility

As AI becomes more embedded in workplace processes, there will be an increased focus on ethical considerations:

- **Responsible AI Usage**: Organizations will need to establish guidelines and policies for the ethical use of AI, particularly regarding data privacy and algorithmic bias. This trend will ensure that AI tools are deployed responsibly, maintaining trust among employees and customers.

- **Transparency in AI Decision-Making**: Businesses will increasingly prioritize transparency in how AI systems make decisions. This focus will involve explaining the algorithms' functioning and ensuring accountability in AI-driven outcomes.

Conclusion

The future of AI holds immense potential to enhance productivity across various domains. As generative AI, NLP, and remote work enhancements continue to evolve, organizations that embrace these technologies will likely gain a competitive edge. However, it is equally important to navigate the ethical landscape surrounding AI to ensure responsible and equitable usage. By staying informed about these emerging trends, businesses and individuals can harness the full power of AI to optimize workflows and drive success in an increasingly dynamic work environment.

Chapter 7: Planning for the Future – Embracing Continuous Growth with AI

Staying Updated on AI Innovations

In a rapidly evolving technological landscape, staying informed about AI innovations is crucial for businesses and individuals alike. Here are some practical steps to keep pace with new developments:

1. **Subscribe to Industry Newsletters**: Sign up for newsletters from reputable sources like TechCrunch, Wired, or specific AI-focused platforms. These outlets often highlight the latest tools, research breakthroughs, and emerging trends.

2. **Participate in Online Communities**: Join forums and social media groups on platforms

like LinkedIn, Reddit, or specialized AI communities. Engaging in discussions with peers can provide insights into how others are utilizing AI and staying ahead of the curve.

3. **Attend Webinars and Conferences**: Look for webinars, workshops, and conferences focused on AI. These events often feature expert speakers sharing their experiences and predictions about future trends. They also provide networking opportunities that can lead to collaborations or mentorships.

4. **Follow Thought Leaders**: Identify and follow influential figures in the AI space, such as researchers, entrepreneurs, and industry analysts. Their insights can offer valuable perspectives on where AI is headed and how to prepare for changes.

5. **Experiment with New Tools**: Regularly test out new AI tools and applications. Many platforms offer free trials, allowing you to explore their features and see how they can enhance your workflows. By being hands-on, you can discover innovative solutions that suit your needs.

Adapting to Future Work Trends with AI Tools

As AI continues to evolve, its impact on various fields will only deepen. Here's how AI is expected to transform content creation, project management, and personalized learning:

- **Content Creation**: The future of content creation will see AI tools becoming more integrated and intuitive. Advanced algorithms will assist not only in generating written content but also in analyzing audience engagement, enabling creators to tailor their messages for maximum impact. Tools will evolve to provide real-time feedback on tone, style, and even emotional resonance, helping writers connect more effectively with their audiences.

- **Project Management**: AI will revolutionize project management by automating repetitive tasks, predicting project risks, and optimizing resource allocation. For example, AI-driven platforms will analyze team performance data to recommend workflow adjustments, ensuring that projects stay on track. Predictive analytics will enable managers to anticipate bottlenecks before they occur, leading to smoother project execution.

- **Personalized Learning**: The landscape of education and professional development will be reshaped by AI. Future learning platforms will leverage machine learning to analyze an individual's learning style, pace, and interests, creating customized curricula that adapt in real-time. This personalization will enhance knowledge retention and application, allowing learners to achieve their goals more efficiently.

Building a Resilient and Future-Ready Mindset

Embracing AI is not just about adopting new tools; it's about fostering a mindset that values adaptability and growth. Here are some key aspects to consider:

1. **Embrace Lifelong Learning**: Commit to continuous learning and self-improvement. The rapid pace of technological change means that skills can quickly become outdated. Regularly seek out opportunities for professional development, whether through formal education, online courses, or self-study.

2. **Foster a Culture of Innovation**: Encourage creativity and experimentation in your workplace or personal projects. Create an environment where trying new AI tools and techniques is welcomed, and failure is seen as a stepping stone to success.

3. **Be Open to Change**: Cultivate flexibility in your approach to work and technology. Recognize that the tools and processes that work today may evolve, and being open to change will help you navigate transitions smoothly.

4. **Seek Feedback**: Actively solicit feedback from peers, mentors, or team members on your use of AI tools. Constructive criticism can help you refine your approach and discover new ways to leverage technology effectively.

5. **Align AI Adoption with Values**: As you integrate AI into your workflows, ensure that your choices align with your personal and professional values. Consider the ethical implications of the tools you use and strive to foster transparency and fairness in AI applications.

Planning for the future with AI is not merely about adopting the latest technologies; it's about cultivating a mindset of continuous growth, adaptability, and ethical responsibility. By staying updated on innovations, adapting to future work trends, and building resilience, individuals and organizations can harness the full potential of AI to drive productivity and success in an ever-changing landscape. Embracing these principles will empower you to navigate the complexities of the future with confidence and purpose, ensuring that you remain competitive in a world increasingly defined by AI.

Conclusion

Summing Up Key Takeaways

Throughout this exploration of AI-powered productivity, we've uncovered the myriad ways in which AI can enhance efficiency and effectiveness across a diverse range of tasks. From automating repetitive workflows and streamlining content creation to facilitating personalized learning experiences, AI tools are proving indispensable in today's fast-paced work environment. These technologies empower individuals and organizations alike to achieve their goals with unprecedented speed and accuracy. By integrating AI into daily operations, professionals can focus on higher-level strategic thinking and creative problem-solving, ultimately elevating their work and contributing to a more innovative workplace culture.

The Long-Term Benefits of AI-Driven Productivity

The long-term benefits of adopting AI-driven productivity strategies extend far beyond immediate efficiency gains. Organizations that consistently leverage AI tools are better positioned to adapt to market changes, respond to customer needs, and stay ahead of the competition. Furthermore, AI's ability to analyze vast amounts of data allows for informed decision-making that can lead to significant cost savings and resource optimization. On an individual level, embracing AI can foster a healthier work-life balance. By automating mundane tasks, professionals can allocate more time to personal pursuits and professional development, ultimately enhancing their overall quality of life. As AI continues to evolve, those who harness its potential will find themselves not only thriving in their careers but also enjoying a more fulfilling lifestyle.

Final Thoughts on Integrating AI Seamlessly

As we conclude this journey into the realm of AI-powered productivity, we encourage you to approach your integration of these technologies with confidence and curiosity. Whether you are just beginning to explore AI tools or are looking to deepen your existing knowledge, remember that the path to successful AI adoption is one of continuous learning and adaptation. Start small by identifying specific areas in your workflow that could benefit from AI and gradually expand your toolkit as you gain experience.

Take the time to experiment with various AI applications, seek out training resources, and engage with communities of like-minded individuals who share your interest in leveraging AI for productivity. Each step you take toward incorporating AI into your daily routine is a step toward greater innovation and efficiency. Embrace the challenges that come with learning new technologies; they are opportunities for growth and improvement.

Ultimately, the future of work is not about AI replacing human effort but rather about augmenting it— enhancing our capabilities, streamlining our processes, and enabling us to focus on what truly matters. With AI as your ally, you can navigate the complexities of the modern workplace with agility and assurance, paving the way for a more productive, balanced, and successful future.

As you embark on or continue your AI journey, remain open to the possibilities that lie ahead. The integration of AI into your work will not only help you stay competitive in an increasingly digital world but also empower you to shape your own path in this exciting new era of productivity.

Appendix

Glossary of Common AI Terms

1. **Artificial Intelligence (AI)**: A branch of computer science that focuses on creating systems capable of performing tasks that typically require human intelligence, such as understanding language, recognizing patterns, and making decisions.

2. **Machine Learning (ML)**: A subset of AI that involves algorithms that allow computers to learn from and make predictions based on data without explicit programming.

3. **Natural Language Processing (NLP)**: A field of AI that focuses on the interaction between computers and humans through natural language, enabling machines to understand, interpret, and respond to human language.

4. **Predictive Analytics**: Techniques that use statistical algorithms and machine learning to identify the likelihood of future outcomes based on historical data.

5. **Generative AI**: A type of AI that can generate new content, such as images, text, or music, based on patterns learned from existing data.

6. **Neural Networks**: A series of algorithms that mimic the operations of the human brain to

recognize relationships in data, often used in deep learning.

7. **Automation**: The use of technology to perform tasks with minimal human intervention, often enhancing efficiency and reducing the likelihood of errors.

8. **Data Privacy**: The aspect of information technology that deals with the proper handling of sensitive data, including how it is collected, stored, and shared.

9. **Chatbot**: An AI program that simulates human conversation through voice or text interactions, often used in customer service to assist users.

10. **Computer Vision**: A field of AI that enables computers to interpret and make decisions based on visual data, such as images and videos.

Resource Guide for AI Tools and Tutorials

To help you navigate the world of AI and maximize productivity in your workplace, here's a curated list of resources, tools, and platforms that can aid your exploration and implementation of AI technologies.

AI Tools

1. **Writing and Content Creation**

   o **ChatGPT**: A conversational AI tool that helps generate ideas, content, and even complete articles. Ideal for overcoming writer's block.

- o **Jasper**: An AI writing assistant that excels in creating marketing copy and engaging content.

- o **Sudowrite**: A tool tailored for novelists, enhancing narrative creation and character development.

2. **Data Analysis and Visualization**

- o **Tableau**: A powerful data visualization tool that enables users to create interactive, shareable dashboards.

- o **MonkeyLearn**: A user-friendly platform for text analysis and machine learning, great for businesses looking to analyze customer feedback or survey results.

3. **Project Management**

- o **Trello**: A flexible project management tool that uses boards, lists, and cards to organize tasks, enhanced by automation features.

- o **Asana**: A collaborative platform that helps teams track their work and manage projects, with AI capabilities for task prioritization.

4. **Design and Visual Creativity**

- **Canva**: An intuitive graphic design tool that includes AI features for creating stunning visuals for marketing materials.

- **DALL-E**: An AI model that generates unique images from textual descriptions, useful for creating custom graphics.

5. **Learning and Skill Development**

- **Coursera**: Offers AI-driven recommendations for courses based on your interests and previous learning.

- **LinkedIn Learning**: Provides a wide range of video courses, enhanced by AI algorithms that suggest relevant content based on career goals.

6. **Research Assistance**

- **Elicit**: A tool designed for researchers to facilitate literature reviews by summarizing papers and generating citations.

- **Scholarcy**: An AI-powered summarizer that helps users quickly grasp the key points of academic papers.

Additional Resources and Recommended Platforms

1. **Online Learning Platforms**

- **edX**: Provides free online courses from universities, including topics on AI and machine learning.

- **Udacity**: Offers nano-degree programs in AI and data science, focusing on practical applications and real-world projects.

2. **Community and Forums**

- **Kaggle**: A community for data scientists and machine learning practitioners to share insights, code, and datasets.

- **AI Dungeon**: A creative writing platform powered by AI, where users can collaborate on storytelling.

3. **Blogs and Publications**

- **Towards Data Science**: A Medium publication with articles on AI, machine learning, and data science, suitable for both beginners and experts.

- **OpenAI Blog**: Features updates and insights on the latest advancements in AI technologies, written by industry leaders.

4. **Podcasts**

- **AI Alignment Podcast**: Discusses the implications of AI development and its societal impact, featuring interviews with researchers and thought leaders.

- The **TWIML AI Podcast**: Focuses on the latest developments in machine learning and artificial intelligence through interviews and discussions.

5. **Books**

- **"Artificial Intelligence: A Guide to Intelligent Systems" by Michael Negnevitsky**: A comprehensive introduction to AI principles and applications.

- **"Deep Learning" by Ian Goodfellow, Yoshua Bengio, and Aaron Courville**: A foundational text for understanding deep learning methodologies.

Acknowledgement

I extend my heartfelt appreciation to my husband for his unwavering support and selfless dedication throughout the creation of this book, "**AI-Powered Productivity: Maximizing Efficiency and Success in the Modern Workplace**." His tireless efforts behind the scenes have been instrumental in shaping this material into a work that I hope will be both enriching and worthwhile for our readers. His encouragement, patience, and invaluable insights have truly made a difference, and I am deeply grateful for his partnership in this endeavor.

About The Author

Nena Buenaventura is a dedicated leader with a rich and diverse career spanning healthcare and business. Her unwavering commitment to service first manifested in healthcare, where she spearheaded departments, empowering patients to reclaim their health and independence. Driven by an entrepreneurial spirit, she transitioned to the business world, deepening her understanding of finance and entrepreneurship. Nena's multifaceted journey culminates in her prolific writing, where she shares her knowledge and insights across a range of disciplines, connecting with readers on a personal and intellectual level.

Through her impactful work in healthcare, business, and writing, Nena continues to make a lasting difference in the world.

Books List in Amazon Authored by Nena Buenaventura

https://www.amazon.com/s?k=nena+buenaventura&crid=3YAQC K674WD5&qid=1730203709&sprefix=Nena+Buen%2Caps%2C399 &ref=sr_pg_1